DOG

woof woof

LIFE CYCLES

Words that look like **this** can be found in the glossary on page 24.

©2018
Book Life
King's Lynn
Norfolk PE30 4LS

ISBN: 978-1-78637-236-9

Written by:
Holly Duhig
Edited by:
Kirsty Holmes
Designed by:
Danielle Jones

A catalogue record for this book
is available from the British Library.

DOG

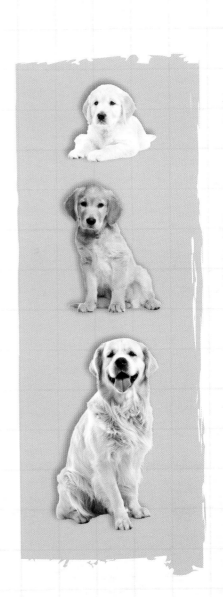

WHAT IS A LIFE CYCLE?

All animals, plants and humans go through different stages of their life as they grow and change. This is called a life cycle.

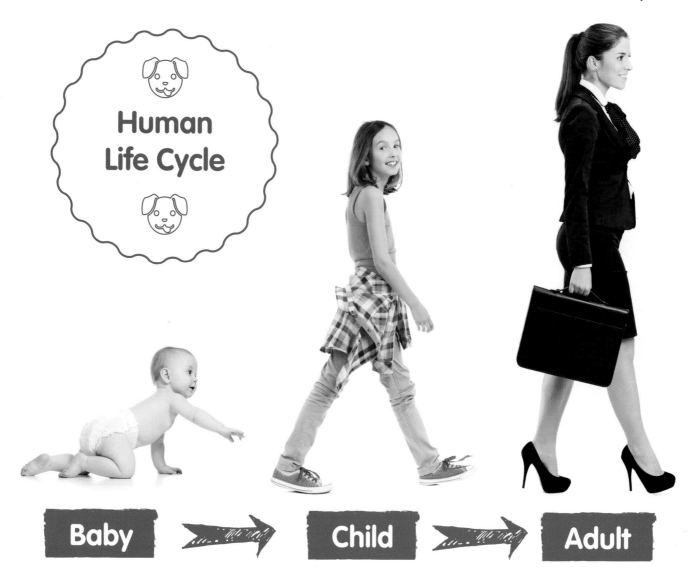

Human Life Cycle

Baby ➤ Child ➤ Adult

WHAT IS A DOG?

A dog is a **species** of **mammal**. They like to live in groups with humans or other dogs. This is why they make such good pets.

5

PUPPIES

Puppies are an adult dog's **young**. A female dog will be **pregnant** for between 58 to 68 days, before giving birth to her puppies.

This dog is ready to give birth.

A group of puppies from the same mother is called a litter.

Once they are born, puppies will spend most of their time sleeping and drinking their mother's milk. This helps them to grow.

GROWING PUPPIES

When puppies are born, they can't hear, see or smell. They stay close to their mother until they have grown bigger and stronger.

Puppies are born without teeth.

Just like human babies, puppies can't walk straight away.
They begin to walk once their legs have grown big enough
to support their bodies.

CHANGING PUPPIES

By the time a puppy is three weeks old, it will have grown a set of teeth. Puppies like to chew on things so their teeth grow stronger.

After a few weeks, puppies **develop** a sense of smell. This sense is very important to them. Puppies use smells to understand the world around them.

Scientists believe a dog's sense of smell is between 1,000 – 10,000 times better than human's!

DOGS

Puppies become dogs once they are fully grown. Most puppies become adult dogs when they reach one year of age.

Adult dogs need plenty of exercise in order to stay healthy. Dogs are **sociable** animals so they love to meet other dogs at the park.

Dogs love to play catch!

DIFFERENT BREEDS

There are many different **breeds** of dog. Many of these breeds have been chosen by humans to do special jobs based on their skills and **characteristics**.

Border collies are often known as sheep dogs because they are used by farmers to round up sheep. They are one of the cleverest dog breeds.

Border Collie

Labradors are easy to **train**. Because of this, they are often used as **guide dogs** by people who are blind.

Labrador

This dog is helping her owner to cross the street.

Bloodhounds have an amazing sense of smell. Police officers use the bloodhound's sense of smell to track down criminals and missing people.

Bloodhound

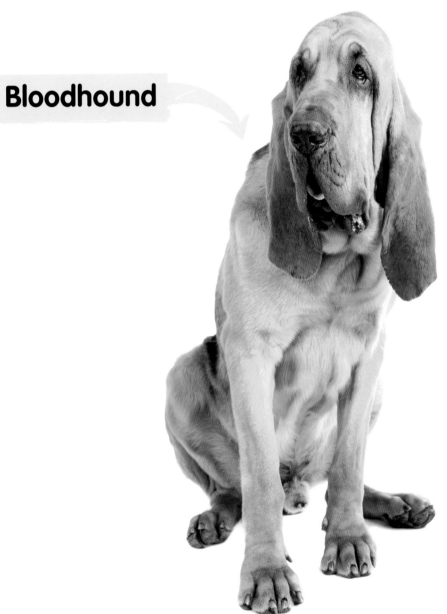

DOG FACTS

Dogs and wolves are related. They belong to the same family
in the animal kingdom.

Dogs mainly sweat from their paws.

WORLD RECORD BREAKERS

Shortest Dog in the World

This record is held by Milly the Chihuahua. She is only 9.65 centimetres tall!

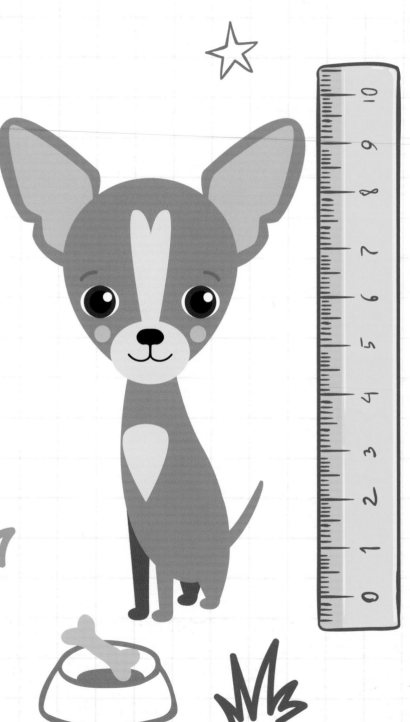

Largest Litter of Puppies

The largest litter of puppies ever recorded was born on the 29th of November, 2004. There were 24 puppies in the litter.

LIFE CYCLE OF A DOG

1 A female dog gives birth to a litter of puppies.

2 The puppies drink their mother's milk until they are strong enough to explore the world.

3 The puppies grow teeth and their hearing, eyesight and sense of smell improves.

4 The puppies become adult dogs and have puppies of their own.

LIFE CYCLES

GET EXPLORING!

Do you, or any of your friends, own a dog? What breed is it?
If it's easy to train, why not teach it to sit or give paw?